Learning To Love God's Way

Dr. Rick Kurnow

ISBN-13: 978-1478300779

ISBN-10: 1478300779

Dedication

To : Yeshua (Jesus) The one who loved me first.
The one who taught me to love His way.
Thank you for putting the Love of God in my heart
by Ruach Ha Kodesh (The Holy Spirit)

I Am Love

"And we have known and believed the love that God has for us. God is love, and he who abides in love abides in God, and God in him." 1 John 4:16

Now – today is the day of salvation. Many souls are weighing in the balance. Who will go for Me? Who will tell them that I Am the way, the truth and the life? Bring them to Me – for I Am gentle, loving and kind and I will embrace them. I will heal them. I will comfort them. I Am a just God and I Am the king and ruler of the universe. But I Am love. I created love. It is the very essence of who I Am. Love is the highest and best and I will lavish you and My people with My love. Look to Me for all good things. I will not withhold it from you. But I freely give of Myself to you. Be filled with all the fullness of God. Be filled with My love.

Table of Contents

All scripture quotations are from the New King James Version unless otherwise noted

Introduction

Learning To Love

Many people do not know how to truly love. When a person does not walk in true love their relationship with God and people are affected. The Bible holds the key to the treasure box that contains the love of God. This book shares insights from the scripture that will revolutionize your understanding of love and your ability to love God and others. Learning to love God's way is the only way a person can succeed in life. This book will impact your friendships, marriage, even your church or congregation. Be filled with all the fullness of God. Be filled with His love.

Chapter 1

What Is Love?

The word 'love' is so freely used in so many contexts that it can mean so many different things to different people.
It is used in so many forms that it loses its meaning and impact. I hear myself saying things like "I love Chinese food" or "I loved that movie". The enjoyment we get from something can make us feel good but it is not the true meaning of love. So what is love?

The Bible was originally written in Hebrew and Greek. Both languages use different words to describe love which paints a clearer picture of what love is.

In ancient Greek there were several different words for love and affection, the four most significant are:

1. agape - voluntary love
2. phileos - emotional love
3. eros - physical or sensual love
4. storge - natural affection

The New Testament was written in Koine Greek, which was the common language of the people of the time (whereas ancient Greek was more of an academic language). There are two primary Greek words that are translated 'love' in the New Testament:

1. Phileo : brotherly or love between family, an emotional love

2. Agape : supreme love, an unconditional love, always voluntary, especially when referring to the love of God.

There are actually several Hebrew words in the Old Testament that in some translations have been translated 'love' Some words isolated to one scripture and some more widely used.

The Hebrew word (*ra'yāh*) occurs only in the Song of Solomon with reference to a "female companion, girlfriend, beloved"

The word (*dōd*) beloved, lover; in other verses in the Song of Soolomon, as well as in a couple of verses in Ezekiel and in one verse in Proverbs, the word means "love (lust)"

the word (*khōbēb*), which occurs only in Deuteronomy 33:3.wherein the text speaks of God loving the people

Also rare (occurring only in Jeremiah and in Ezekiel) is the verb (*'ōg^e bīm*) : to desire sensuously. (occurring only in Ezekiel) is (*^agābāh*) : passion.

Another rare word is (*yādīd*) 1. beloved; 2. adjective lovely; a related word is (*y^e dīdōt*) = love (song) Psalm 45:1.rendered "wedding" (song) in some versions.

The usual word used for "love" in the Hebrew Bible is the verb (*'āhēb*) other forms of the word (*'ahab, 'ōhab,* and *'ah^e bāh*) "to like" as well as "to love"

Then there is the most rendered word in the Hebrew Bible (*khesed*). joint obligation between relatives, friends, host and guest, master and servant; closeness, solidarity, loyalty; lasting loyalty, faithfulness protection favour of the king

- in God's relationship with the people or an individual faithfulness, goodness, graciousness

- the individual actions resulting from solidarity: godly action, achievements [...] proofs of mercy

The word (*khesed*) is translated "love", "loving", and "loving-kindness" in various scriptures.

You don't have to memorize all these words in Greek and Hebrew to understand love. The point is this: love has so many meanings. Each person has a different perception from another.

Agape – The Highest Form of Love

The main focus of this book will be on Agape Love. Supreme love, an unconditional love, always voluntary, especially when referring to the love of God. As far as I am concerned this form of love is the most necessary love in a person's life. If you begin to understand this type of love you will begin to experience the highest form of love in the universe. Agape love comes from God and is freely given to all who will receive. The people who learn to love God's way will have successful friendships, marriages, churches, jobs and more. The Apostle Paul clearly states in 1 Corinthians 13:8 "Love never fails."

There are many things we learn in life. But the most important thing to learn is to love God's way. This type of love will equip you to face anything that comes your way. Circumstances change and people change, but The Love of God remains constant and sure and will never change. People want to be loved and need to learn how to love and yet they look for love in all the wrong places and they settle for inferior counterfeits of love. Are you looking for love in all the wrong places? Are you settling for an inferior counterfeit love? It looks like love, it sounds like love, but is it really love?

We are going to look into the treasure chest of the Word of God. There are so many wonderful scriptures that teach us about the love that comes from God. As we take each scripture from the treasure chest and begin to examine it we will discover that we have had a priceless treasure right in front of us. The answer and key to our relationships and true happiness in this life. God has it all for you and me. Let's discover these precious truths together and I guarantee it will change your life radically for good.

Where Do I Start?

The first step to understanding God's love and receiving His love is to come into a relationship with Him. There are many religious people in this world . They know a lot about God , but they do not know God. How do you know God?

A very famous portion of scripture that many people have heard is: **John 3:16-17** " For **God so loved the world** *that He gave His only begotten Son, that whoever believes in Him should not perish but have everlasting life.17 For God* *did not send His Son into the world to condemn the world, but that the world through Him might be saved."*

This scripture clearly shows us that God loves all the people of this world. And because He does, He sent His son. His son is Yeshua Ha Mashiach (Jesus The Messiah) He came to save us. When we believe in Him we will not perish but we will have everlasting life. He did not come to condemn us but to save us. So are you saved?

Romans 5:6-10 *"For when we were still without strength, in due time Christ died for the ungodly.7 For scarcely for a righteous man will one die; yet perhaps for a good man someone would even dare to die.8 But **God demonstrates His own love toward us,** in that while we were still sinners, Christ died for us.9 Much more then, **having now been justified by His blood, we shall be saved from wrath through Him."***

Jesus took the punishment of our sins, our failures. He took our place and paid the price. God demonstrated His love toward you and me. Love is not just words. "I Love You" how many times have you heard that but it was just words. Well God said "I Love You" by giving His only son and allowing Him to take our place on the cross. We should have died on the cross for our own sins. But Jesus took our place.

1 John 4:19 *"We love Him because He first loved us"*

He took the first step towards us to restore our relationship with Him. Now we need to take our first step towards Him by receiving His salvation.

Romans 10:8-13 *But what does it say? "The word is near you, in your mouth and in your heart" (that is, the word of faith which we preach):9 that **if you confess with your***

mouth the Lord Jesus and believe in your heart that God has raised Him from the dead, you will be saved.10 For with the heart one believes unto righteousness, and with the mouth confession is made unto salvation.11 For the Scripture says, "Whoever believes on Him will not be put to shame." 12 For there is no distinction between Jew and Greek, for the same Lord over all is rich to all who call upon Him.13 For "whoever calls on the name of the LORD shall be saved."

If you have not been saved yet, why not now? Here is a prayer you can pray. It is not a formula or a ritual. But an example for you to pray from your heart. If you will pray this from your heart you will begin a relationship with God that will open the door to experience the highest form of love in the universe.

> *"Father, I know that I have broken your laws and my sins have separated me from you. I am truly sorry, and now I want to turn away from my past sinful life toward you. Please forgive me, and help me avoid sinning again. I believe that your son, Jesus Christ died for my sins, was resurrected from the dead, is alive, and hears my prayer. I invite Jesus to become the Lord of my life, to rule and reign in my heart from this day forward. Please send your Holy Spirit to help me obey You, and to do Your will for the rest of my life. I ask that the Holy Spirit would fill me with the Love of God. In Jesus' name I pray, Amen."*

How does Jesus come into your heart and life? How does He live inside of you? He comes into your life by His Holy Spirit. Be filled with the Holy Spirit and you will be filled with His love.

Romans 5:5 *"Now hope does not disappoint, because **the love of God has been poured out in our hearts by the Holy Spirit** who was given to us."*

Chapter 2

The Royal Law

God gave 613 laws through Moses. Many people thought that maybe God was cruel to give His people so many laws that no one could keep. It seemed to give the appearance that God was setting His people up to fail.

Think about the Ten Commandments. No one I know and no one you know has been able to keep all the ten commandments perfectly. Jesus was the only one who ever lived that actually kept and fulfilled all the law. So why did He give us the law if He knew we could not keep it?

Galatians 3:19-25

"What purpose then does the law serve? **It was added because of transgressions,** *till the Seed should come to whom the promise was made; and it was appointed through angels by the hand of a mediator. 20 Now a mediator does not mediate for one only, but God is one. 21 Is the law then against the promises of God? Certainly not! For if there had been a law given which could have given life, truly righteousness would have been by the law. 22 But* **the Scripture has confined all under sin,** *that the promise by faith in Jesus Christ might be given to those who believe. 23 But* **before faith came, we were kept under guard by the law,** *kept for the faith which would afterward be revealed. 24 Therefore* **the law was our tutor to bring us to Christ,** *that*

we might be justified by faith. 25 ***But after faith has come, we are no longer under a tutor.***"

The law was given to us as a measuring stick. God's standard of holiness and righteousness far exceeds our holiness and righteousness. If we did not have the law we would have nothing to measure ourselves against and nothing to prove to us that we fall short of God's standards. And nothing to tutor us in the right direction towards His standards.

Romans 3:10
"As it is written: ***"There is none righteous, no, not one"***

Romans 3:23
"For all have sinned and fall short of the glory of God"

The law proves to you and me that we are sinners. God gave us the law to show us that we have sinned . It was not a cruel plan to set us up to fail. It was actually given as a protection to guard us and to keep us from self –destructing because of our sinful nature.

When you put your faith in the finished work of Jesus Christ your life is transformed and a different law goes into effect. The law of the Spirit. The laws of Moses brought condemnation and proof that we needed to be saved. But once we are saved God fulfills the righteous requirement of the law by putting His Spirit in you.

Romans 8:2-5
"For ***the law of the Spirit*** *of life in Christ Jesus has made me free from the law of sin and death. 3 For what the law could not do in that it was weak through the flesh, God did by sending His own Son in the likeness of sinful flesh, on account of sin: He condemned sin in the flesh, 4* ***that the righteous requirement of the law might be fulfilled in us***

who do not walk according to the flesh but according to the Spirit."

2 Corinthians 5:21
"For He made Him who knew no sin to be sin for us, that we might become the righteousness of God in Him."

A Higher Law, A Better Law, A Royal Law

Out of 613 laws of Moses there are 2 that fulfill all the law.

Matthew 22:37-40
37 Jesus said to him, **"'You shall love the LORD your God with all your heart, with all your soul, and with all your mind.'** *38 This is the first and great commandment.39 And the second is like it:* **'You shall love your neighbor as yourself.'** *40* **On these two commandments hang all the Law and the Prophets."**

Loving God and loving others fulfills the law. It is that simple yet it is so deep. God is not asking you to keep 613 laws. He is only asking you to keep two. And He has given you His Spirit to help you accomplish this. If you learn to walk according to the Royal Law your life will never be the same. The best part is that "Love" is the key to fulfilling this law.

James 2:8
8 If you really fulfill **the royal law** *according to the Scripture, "You shall love your neighbor as yourself," you do well;*

That is nice to know but how do we get this love and how do we walk in it? The Royal Law can only be fulfilled by the Holy Spirit baptizing you in the love of God.

Romans 5:5 *"Now hope does not disappoint, because **the love of God has been poured out in our hearts by the Holy Spirit** who was given to us."*

The fruit that comes out of your life will not be your fruit, but instead the fruit of the Spirit. Do you want to learn how to love God's way? Then you must walk in the Spirit.. Be filled with the Holy Spirit and the fruit of love will flow out of your life and you will fulfill the Royal Law.

Galatians 5:16-24

16 I say then: **Walk in the Spirit, and you shall not fulfill the lust of the flesh.** 17 For the flesh lusts against the Spirit, and the Spirit against the flesh; and these are contrary to one another, so that you do not do the things that you wish. 18 But **if you are led by the Spirit, you are not under the law**. 19 Now the works of the flesh are evident, which are: adultery, fornication, uncleanness, lewdness, 20 idolatry, sorcery, hatred, contentions, jealousies, outbursts of wrath, selfish ambitions, dissensions, heresies, 21 envy, murders, drunkenness, revelries, and the like; of which I tell you beforehand, just as I also told you in time past, that those who practice such things will not inherit the kingdom of God. 22 But **the fruit of the Spirit is love**, joy, peace, longsuffering, kindness, goodness, faithfulness, 23 gentleness, self-control. **Against such there is no law.**

The main fruit of the Spirit is love. All the other fruits are born out of that love. When you walk in this love you are no longer under the former law. In fact there is no need for the law when you walk in agape love. (God's supreme love, an unconditional love, always voluntary)

Why is it that love fulfills the requirements of the law?

Romans 13:8-10
8 *Owe no one anything except to love one another, for **he who loves another has fulfilled the law**. 9 For the commandments, "You shall not commit adultery," "You shall not murder," "You shall not steal," "You shall not bear false witness," "You shall not covet," and if there is any other commandment, are all summed up in this saying, namely, "You shall love your neighbor as yourself." 10 **Love does no harm to a neighbor; therefore love is the fulfillment of the law.***

That's right. "he who loves another has fulfilled the law" and "Love does no harm to a neighbor; therefore love is the fulfillment of the law." If you love someone you will not commit adultery, you will not murder, steal, lie or covet. When you love there is no need for the law.

Thank God that He is the one who can give you the love you need. He has an endless supply. It will never run dry. People can do a lot of nice things on their own. But when they walk in the highest form of love, this love can only come from God. When you put your faith in the finished work of Jesus Christ then what you build upon that foundation must be built by God. Nothing else is acceptable to Him. So what is acceptable to God?

Ephesians 5:8-10

8 For you were once darkness, but now you are light in the Lord. Walk as children of light 9(for the fruit of the Spirit is in all goodness, righteousness, and truth), 10 finding out what is acceptable to the Lord.

Only the fruit of the Spirit is what is acceptable to God. God's love: The fruit of the Spirit, is in all goodness , righteousness and truth.

Chapter 3

God is Love

1 John 4:7,8

Beloved, let us love one another, for love is of God; and ***everyone who loves is born of God and knows God.*** *8 He who does not love does not know God,* ***for God is love.***

What does the statement "God is love" mean? On the surface it could appear that God is the principle of love. Some people would interpret this to mean that love is God. Actually , God is the full representation and manifestation of all that love is. The more you know God, the more you will know love. The love that comes from God is so vast.

Ephesians 3:17-19

17 that Christ may dwell in your hearts through faith; that you, being rooted and grounded in love,18 may be able to comprehend with all the saints what is the width and length and depth and height --19 ***to know the love of Christ which passes knowledge;*** *that you may be filled with all* ***the fullness of God.***

15

Our desire should always be to know God more and to know His love. To know the width, length, depth and height of His love. *"To know the love of Christ which passes knowledge"* seems to be a contradictory statement. How can you know something that passes knowledge? You could not in this life exhaust all that there is to know about His love. Yet the more you know of His love, the more you will know and experience the fullness of all that God is. Be filled with all the fullness of God. Be filled with His love.

1 John 2:5-6
5 But whoever keeps His word, truly the love of God is perfected in him. By this we know that we are in Him.6 He who says he abides in Him **ought himself also to walk just as He walked.**

If you are walking close to Jesus you will walk just as He walked. He walked in love and you can walk in love. Many people say, "Yeah, but I am not Jesus. He is divine and I am only human ." That is true, but Jesus lives in you by the Holy Spirit. Draw closer to God and you will begin to walk just as He walked. That love that is shed abroad in your heart by the Holy Spirit will begin to manifest from your life. *"Everyone who loves is born of God and knows God."*

The Character of Love

God's character emanates love. When you look at God you see true love. I described agape love as being God's supreme love, an unconditional love, always voluntary.

Supreme Love

His love is supreme. It is above every form of love in this universe. His love can be applied to every aspect of living. In fact it must be applied to every aspect of living. Without agape love in your life every relationship will miserably fail. It may give the appearance of love but it will be inferior and a counterfeit to the highest form of love. Why settle for something inferior when you can experience the genuine?

Unconditional Love

God's love is unconditional. What does that mean? Simply put: His love is not based on conditions. It is not based on performance. His love is consistent towards you no matter what has happened , what is happening or what will happen.

Unconditional love can be like a thermostat as compared to a thermometer. A thermostat is set and is always working to keep its environment consistent no matter how much the environment around it changes. But a thermometer is up when it is hot and it is down when it is cold. A thermometer does not change or affect its environment. It is just moved by its environment. Isn't most people's love this way? As long as things are going good in a relationship it is easy to love. But when things change so does our love. Basically most people have conditional love. When you think about it, this type of love is very self centered. If you can meet my needs. If you can make me feel good. If you can show me you appreciate me. Then I will feel loved and then I can love you.

Let's trade in our conditional love for unconditional love. God will give you the love you need to love people 100% even when you are getting nothing back. But why give if you are not going to get anything back? Isn't that a waste of your love? I will let you in on a secret. Actually it is not a secret but most people don't understand the results of walking in unconditional love. "You reap what you sow" The more you give of unconditional love, the more it will come back to you. This is not the motive for giving this type of love, but it is a benefit. It may not come back to you from the person you are directing it to. But it will come back to you from God.

Colossians 3:23-24
"And whatever you do, do it heartily, as to the Lord and not to men,24 knowing that from the Lord you will receive the reward of the inheritance; for you serve the Lord Christ."

Jesus gave His life for you and me even when we didn't care. He was not getting anything back from any of us at the time. In fact even the closest people to him fled from Him. He was all alone. So what drove Him? Why would He allow himself to be beaten, scourged and crucified if He had the power to stop it all? It was unconditional love. He loved you and me so much He was willing to give 100% even when He wasn't getting anything back at the time.

John 15:13
"Greater love has no one than this, than to lay down one's life for his friends."

You don't have to die for others to prove unconditional love. Jesus already did the ultimate act of unconditional love. You will never have to go the extent Jesus did for you. But learning to love God's way means you must learn to walk in unconditional love. Paul the Apostle learned how to love this way. He experienced so many "perils" from people. Yet he so clearly stated unconditional love when he wrote:

2 Corinthians 12:15
"And I will very gladly spend and be spent for your souls; though the more abundantly I love you, the less I am loved."

Voluntary Love

God wants you to give love voluntarily. Not because you have to, or because it is the right thing to do. But because you want to. I remember when I was first saved I was thinking about the tree in the middle of the Garden of Eden. The tree of the knowledge of good and evil. I said to God, "If you had never put that tree in the garden then Adam & Eve would have never sinned and our world would not be in the mess it is in." His reply to me was, "I put that tree in the garden because I wanted them to love Me because they wanted to and not because they had to." God loves us not because He has to. But because He wants to. We should love Him back the same way and love people the same way.

Ephesians 1:4
"just as He chose us in Him before the foundation of the world, that we should be holy and without blame before Him in love."

Chapter 4

Love Forgives

What does it mean to forgive? It means to refrain from imposing punishment on an offender or demanding satisfaction for an offense. To forgive is to grant pardon without harboring resentment.

Most people find it very hard to forgive others. Many people will forgive only if certain conditions have been met to warrant the forgiveness. If the offender apologizes or makes it right. Then maybe they will forgive. Some people hold onto offenses and grudges for years. A small petty offense can build up in a person's imagination and grow into major unforgiveness. Hurt, resentment and anger can grow into a formidable wall that will separate family, friends, marriages and churches for years. All because of unforgiveness and the unwillingness to let go of an offense.

Colossians 3:12-14

*"Therefore, as the elect of God, holy and beloved, put on tender mercies, kindness, humility, meekness, longsuffering; 13 bearing with one another, and **forgiving one another**, if anyone has a complaint against another; **even as Christ forgave you, so you also must do.** 14 But **above all these things put on love**, which is the bond of perfection."*

If you want to walk in love you must learn to forgive or you will never be able to walk in love. You cannot forgive if you don't have love, and you cannot love if you don't forgive.

Forgiveness is a key part in learning to love God's way. Forgiveness requires grace (receiving something you don't deserve) and also mercy (not receiving what you really deserve)

The way Jesus has forgiven you must be the way you forgive others. *"even as Christ forgave you, so you also must do"*
If you could keep this in mind it would be so much easier to forgive others.

So how did Jesus forgive you? Would you say that He forgave you even when you didn't deserve it? The answer is yes. So you must learn to forgive others even when they don't deserve it. That is where grace and mercy comes in. God shows you grace every day. He gives you so much even when you don't deserve it. And He shows you mercy by not giving you what you really deserve, the punishment for your sins. There is a story that Jesus told that clearly shows us why it is so important for us to forgive others even when they don't deserve it.

Read this story carefully and prayerfully.

Matthew 18:23-35

"Therefore the kingdom of heaven is like a certain king who wanted to settle accounts with his servants. 24 And when he had begun to settle accounts, one was brought to him who owed him ten thousand talents. 25 But as he was not able to pay, his master commanded that he be sold, with his wife and children and all that he had, and that payment be made. 26 The servant therefore fell down before him, saying, 'Master, have patience with me, and I will pay you all.' 27 Then the master of that servant was moved with compassion, released him, and forgave him the debt.

28 "But that servant went out and found one of his fellow servants who owed him a hundred denarii; and he laid hands on him and took him by the throat, saying, 'Pay me what you owe!'29 So his fellow servant fell down at his feet and begged him, saying, 'Have patience with me, and I will pay you all.' 30 And he would not, but went and threw him into prison till he should pay the debt.31 So when his fellow servants saw what had been done, they were very grieved, and came and told their master all that had been done.32 Then his master, after he had called him, said to him, 'You wicked servant! I forgave you all that debt because you begged me.33 Should you not also have had compassion on your fellow servant, just as I had pity on you?'34 And his master was angry, and delivered him to the torturers until he should pay all that was due to him. 35 "So My heavenly Father also will do to you if each of you, from his heart, does not forgive his brother his trespasses."

The debt the master in this story forgave was a very big debt. In comparison the debt the fellow servant owed was quite small. Yet the servant could not forgive his fellow servant. God has forgiven us such a great debt. We didn't deserve it but He chose to forgive us because He loves us. Do you think you are ever justified to hold onto an offense with another and be unwilling to forgive and let it go? The answer is no.

Matthew 6:14-15
*14 "For if you forgive men their trespasses, your heavenly Father will also forgive you.15 But **if you do not forgive men their trespasses, neither will your Father forgive your trespasses.***

Unforgiveness is not worth it. First of all God says in many portions of scripture that if you do not forgive others, He will not forgive you. Secondly, unforgiveness holds you in prison while the offender runs free. The reason I say this is because an offense that you keep continues to bring pain and resentment and the loss of a possible healthy relationship with the one who has offended you. It can make you sick physically, mentally, emotionally and spiritually. The other person may never even realized they did what they did or affected you the way they did. So if you can learn to forgive and let things go then you can go on with your life whether the offender ever makes it right with you. They will no longer hold any power over you to hurt you. The offense can only hurt you if you allow it to.

I heard Dr. Larry Lea say this back in the 1980's and I have never forgotten it. When an offense comes. Don't nurse it, Don't curse it, Don't rehearse it, Instead - disperse it, And God will reverse it.

I Don't want to be a doormat

Many people think that if you have to always forgive others you will become a doormat for others to wipe their feet on and be stepped on all the time. Forgiveness does not mean that you have to allow others to continue to do the things that continually hurt and offend you. You can forgive and love someone yet you can draw necessary boundaries. When we allow others to continue wrong behavior at our expense we become what has been termed an enabler. God does not want you to enable others to continue in sin. Love them, forgive them but do not give them opportunity to continue in the offense towards you. I am not saying not to give others second chances and beyond. But I am saying that we should be wise and careful. We should be led by the Holy Spirit and God will show you how to have tough love. A love that is unconditional but not stupid. (yes I did say that).

24

Forgive and Forget

Have you ever heard someone say " I will forgive , but I won't forget." ? Maybe you have said that yourself. If you forgive someone you will let it go. You won't keep holding onto the offense. The offense won't keep holding onto you.

Philippians 3:13-14
*"13 Brethren, I do not count myself to have apprehended; but **one thing I do, forgetting those things which are behind** and reaching forward to those things which are ahead,14 I press toward the goal for the prize of the upward call of God in Christ Jesus. "*

Holding onto past hurts and offenses will hold you back. Forget about them. You can't go back and change the past. What has been done is done. You can learn from the past, but you don't have to keep re-living the past. God forgives us of all our past and He chooses to forget and not use our past to determine our future. Thank God!

One time I was ministering at a Teen Challenge facility. A young man had been hurt and abused by his father. He told me that he only had to forgive his father 490 times according to what Jesus taught. After that he didn't have to forgive him anymore . He showed me : **Matthew 18:21,22**
"Then Peter came to Him and said, "Lord, how often shall my brother sin against me, and I forgive him? Up to seven times?" 22 Jesus said to him, "I do not say to you, up to seven times, but up to seventy times seven. "

I told him that if he was keeping count he never forgave him the first time. Jesus used the term "seventy times seven" not to set the bar on forgiveness, but instead to emphasize we should always forgive.

God will turn evil to good

I have discovered that God can turn what others intend for evil and turn it to good. So you can't lose no matter what others do to you. This principle resonates throughout the scripture. Think of the evil that was done to Joseph. He was sold into Egypt as a slave. God began to prosper him in the house of Potiphar. Then Potiphar's wife lied and accused him of rape. He was thrown in prison. God began to prosper him there. Just when he thought he was going to get out of prison, he ended staying two more years. He could have lived his life in the prison of unforgiveness. He could have dwelled on all the evil that was done to him. But instead he followed God with all his heart and God blessed him and turned what others meant for evil into good. Finally the day came when God promoted him to become one of the greatest leaders in Egypt. The day came when his brothers who had done evil to him bowed before him afraid that Joseph would repay them for the evil they did to him. But instead Joseph responded with love and forgiveness.

Genesis 50:19-21
Joseph said to them ,"Do not be afraid, for am I in the place of God? 20 But as for you, you meant evil against me; but God meant it for good, in order to bring it about as it is this day, to save many people alive."

Don't focus on the offenses. Go on with your life and let God turn what was meant for evil into good. You know He is really good at doing that. He can make all things work together for your good and His glory.

Love people, forgive people and you will be greatly blessed.

Chapter 5

Love God, Love People

Matthew 22:37-40

"37 Jesus said to him, "'You shall love the LORD your God with all your heart, with all your soul, and with all your mind.' 38 This is the first and great commandment. 39 And the second is like it: 'You shall love your neighbor as yourself.' 40 On these two commandments hang all the Law and the Prophets."

The two most important things in life is to learn to love God and love people. If you make this your goal everyday you will enjoy life and you will fulfill your destiny in God.

For some people it is easy to love God because He is so good and He is always looking out for their best interests. For some people it is hard to love God because they feel like He is not there for them or that He has not kept His promises that He made to them. If you understand how much God loves you, then you would never have a hard time loving Him. I hear people make the statement "I am mad at God" do you know what that tells me about a person? It tells me that they are self centered. They are expecting God to serve them on their terms. God is not our servant, we are suppose to be His servant. It tells me they really don't understand who God is. If you truly saw God for who He is you would see that His motive towards you is love. Did you know that He knows what is best for us? It may not appear to us that way. Don't base your love towards God on what you see or feel. The circumstances that surround us are temporary and often do not paint a true picture of God's plan for your life. Often we expect things the way we want it. Many times the way we want it is not the best for us but we can't see it.

Some people say "If God is all loving and all powerful why did He let this happen?" We must understand that we live in a world where God has given people the freedom to choose. Everyone has a free will. Our world is not in the mess it is in because God has failed. It is because man has failed. There six reasons why we suffer in this life.

1. Because of our own choices

2. Because of the choices of others

3. Because of a direct attack by satan or demonic forces against our life.

4. Because God is bringing correction in our lives.

5. Because of original sin that has affected the laws of nature.

6. Sometimes we can't figure out why. Maybe it is because of our own choices, the choices of others, demonic attack, God bringing correction or original sin. Sometimes you just don't know.

There will be times you will not be able to figure out why something is happening. But you can be assured of this, God loves you. He will never leave you or forsake you. He is for you and not against you. He is with you always even to the end of this age. He is in your corner cheering you on.

Romans 8:35-39
*35 Who shall separate us from the love of Christ? Shall tribulation, or distress, or persecution, or famine, or nakedness, or peril, or sword? 36 As it is written: "For Your sake we are killed all day long; We are accounted as sheep for the slaughter." 37 Yet in all these things we are more than conquerors through Him who loved us. 38 For **I am persuaded** that neither death nor life, nor angels nor principalities nor powers, nor things present nor things to come, 39 nor height nor depth, nor any other created thing, shall be able to separate us from the love of God which is in Christ Jesus our Lord.*

Are you persuaded that nothing can separate you from His love? Because He loves us so much we should love Him with all our heart, soul and mind. If you will learn to love Him with everything within you, then you will be able to learn to love people the way that God loves you. God loves you unconditionally. God always forgives you. His love never gives up on you. His love is not based on your performance or what you can do for Him. His love never ends it will go the distance with you. His love endures forever. His love never fails. Let Him fill you with this type of love and you will have no problem loving others the way He loves you.

Love your neighbor as yourself

Romans 13:8-10

"Owe no one anything except to love one another, for he who loves another has fulfilled the law. 9 For the commandments, "You shall not commit adultery," "You shall not murder," "You shall not steal," "You shall not bear false witness," "You shall not covet," and if there is any other commandment, are all summed up in this saying, namely, **"You shall love your neighbor as yourself."** *10 Love does no harm to a neighbor; therefore love is the fulfillment of the law."*

You must first learn how to love yourself before you can love others. Does that mean you should be self-centered? No. It means that you need to see what God sees in you so that you can learn to love others.

1 John 3:20,21

"For if our heart condemns us, God is greater than our heart, and knows all things. 21 Beloved, if our heart does not condemn us, we have confidence toward God."

If your heart is not condemning you then you will have confidence in your relationship with God. You will have the full assurance that He loves you. That He is for you not against you. With this type of confidence you will love yourself and then you will have the ability to love others. You must have a healthy outlook on yourself and who you are in Christ before you can love your neighbor in the right way. *"Love does no harm to a neighbor"* The way that you want others to love you is the way you should love others. If you love yourself you will not hurt yourself. And if you love others you will do no harm to them either.

Luke 6:31

"And just as you want men to do to you, you also do to them likewise."

Matthew 7:12

"Therefore, whatever you want men to do to you, do also to them, for this is the Law and the Prophets."

God is asking you and me to just do two things. Love Him and love others. You don't have to memorize a long list of things you must do. Just do these two things and you will be successful in life and in all your relationships. I am not giving you an instant formula for success. Doing these two things is a way of life. In some instances you will see immediate amazing results. In some situations it will take a lifetime of loving and maybe you will see results from it. Learning to love God's way is a lifestyle that is lived whether you see any results from it or not. Love should always be given freely from the heart whether you get anything out of it or not.

Chapter 6

Love Your Enemies

Matthew 5:43-48

*"You have heard that it was said, 'You shall love your neighbor and hate your enemy.' 44 But I say to you, **love your enemies, bless those who curse you, do good to those who hate you, and pray for those who spitefully use you and persecute you,** 45 that you may be sons of your Father in heaven; for He makes His sun rise on the evil and on the good, and sends rain on the just and on the unjust. 46 For if you love those who love you, what reward have you? Do not even the tax collectors do the same? 47 And if you greet your brethren only, what do you do more than others? Do not even the tax collectors do so? 48 Therefore you shall be perfect, just as your Father in heaven is perfect.*

What is an enemy? An enemy is one that is antagonistic to another; one seeking to injure, overthrow, or harm another. A hostile unit or force . So why would God ask us to love an enemy? Why would He ask you to bless those who curse you and to do good to those who hate you? Why would He want you to pray for those who spitefully use you and persecute you? These are all good questions. There are many scriptures that can help us understand why He tells us to do this.

Let's take a look at the scripture you just read. Some of the reasons are mentioned in this portion of scripture.

Matthew 5:45-48

"45 that you may be sons of your Father in heaven; for He makes His sun rise on the evil and on the good, and sends rain on the just and on the unjust. 46 For if you love those who love you, what reward have you? Do not even the tax collectors do the same? 47 And if you greet your brethren only, what do you do more than others? Do not even the tax collectors do so? 48 Therefore you shall be perfect, just as your Father in heaven is perfect."

He clearly says that when you do these things you prove that you are a child of God. When you act like Him it proves you belong to Him. He loves the whole world. Not just a select group. He loves all people. He doesn't love their sin and the evil they commit, But he loves them. He is also saying that if you only love those who love you back what reward do you have? Basically that is saying that your love can be conditional , shallow and is self –centered instead of being unconditional. But if you are His child then you should love all people like He loves people. This is called perfect love. That is why you will be perfect just as your Father in heaven is perfect.

Romans 12:17-21

*17 **Repay no one evil for evil**. Have regard for good things in the sight of all men. 18 If it is possible, as much as depends on you, live peaceably with all men. 19 Beloved, **do not avenge yourselves**, but rather give place to wrath; for it is written, **"Vengeance is Mine, I will repay,"** says the Lord.*

20 Therefore "If your enemy is hungry, feed him; If he is thirsty, give him a drink; ***For in so doing you will heap coals of fire on his head."** 21 Do not be overcome by evil, but **overcome evil with good.***

When you repay evil for evil you are stooping to the same level of the one who is doing evil. It is not your place to retaliate for what has been done to you or others. God clearly states that vengeance is His. He has the ability to take care of your enemy. He will repay them for all they have done. He is far more capable than you are to deal with your enemies. Remember "you reap what you sow" No one gets away with anything even though it may appear that way. I suggest you read Psalm 73.

When you love and bless your enemy. When you pray for your enemy. When you do good to your enemy you actually defeat your enemy. First by doing this you take the power they are trying to have over you away from them. And also you "heap coals of fire on his head". This means you prove that you are better than them. Stronger, more secure and fearless. Many people interpret loving your enemies as weakness. They think that you are weak and passive resulting in your demise. That is not true. It actually proves that you trust God who is all powerful and well able to take care of your enemies. It proves that you believe that God can work all things together for your good and His glory.

Loving your enemies does not mean that you allow your enemy to harm you and the ones you care about. It does not mean that you passively stand by while your enemy takes advantage of you. Yet many interpret that if they must love and forgive those that seek our harm then they must allow them to do whatever they want to you and the ones you care about and you just have to take it and then forgive them. On the contrary we must remove ourselves from situations that would bring harm to us and those around us. God does not require you to be abused in the name of love.

Matthew 10:16
"Behold, I send you out as sheep in the midst of wolves. Therefore be wise as serpents and harmless as doves."

God wants you to use wisdom. There are wolves. There are even wolves in sheep's clothing.

Matthew 7:15-16
"Beware of false prophets, who come to you in sheep's clothing, but inwardly they are ravenous wolves.16 You will know them by their fruits."

Be wise , know who you are dealing with and what you are dealing with. But always operate in love.

Luke 6:27-36
"But I say to you who hear: Love your enemies, do good to those who hate you,28 bless those who curse you, and pray for those who spitefully use you.29 To him who strikes you on the one cheek, offer the other also. And from him who takes away your cloak, do not withhold your tunic either.30 Give to everyone who asks of you. And from him who takes away your goods do not ask them back.31 And just as you want men to do to you, you also do to them likewise. 32 "But if you love those who love you, what credit is that to you? For even sinners love those who love them.33 And if you do good to those who do good to you, what credit is that to you? For even sinners do the same.34 And if you lend to those from

whom you hope to receive back, what credit is that to you? For even sinners lend to sinners to receive as much back.35 But love your enemies, do good, and lend, hoping for nothing in return; and your reward will be great, and you will be sons of the Most High. For He is kind to the unthankful and evil.36 Therefore be merciful, just as your Father also is merciful.

Most people when they read Jesus' words *"To him who strikes you on the one cheek, offer the other also."* They immediately think that this type of response is weak. Why should I stand there and take abuse and then let them do it to me again by turning my other cheek? Jesus wasn't telling His disciples that they should stand around and be abused. He was trying to teach his disciples love instead of revenge. They were to follow his example in returning good for evil. When He said *"And from him who takes away your cloak, do not withhold your tunic either."* He wasn't saying that we should let people steal from us and if they do give them some more. He was teaching us that when people steal from us they really can't steal from us. Things are things and God will always restore to you more than what has been stolen from you.

Matthew 10:28

" And do not fear those who kill the body but cannot kill the soul. But rather fear Him who is able to destroy both soul and body in hell. "

Whatever evil people do to you they will never succeed. They can try to hurt you and steal from you but they cannot destroy your soul. You belong to Jesus. You can lose everything you have but He will never leave you or forsake you.

John 16:33
"These things I have spoken to you, that in Me you may have peace. In the world you will have tribulation; but be of good cheer, I have overcome the world."

We have a superior and better way to fight back. The way we fight back and defeat our enemies is different from the tactics our enemies use. We fight with love.

Love as a weapon

Did you know that love can be a weapon? Our biggest enemy is satan and his demons. How do we fight the devil? I hear people yell and scream at the devil. They shout in anger. With hatred they want to go and punch out a devil if they could. These type of emotions the devil understands. He is the author of hate and anger. He feeds on these things. Why would you want to feed the very thing you hate?

The devil does not understand love. So how can he fight it? If you have a weapon your enemy does not understand then they will not know how to fight it. The devil does not understand love. He never will. So he is at a disadvantage when you operate in love. The devil wants to destroy your relationships, your family, your marriage, your church and your job. If you operate in love he has no weapon that can come against you and destroy these things. When you don't know what to do. Walk in love. Love conquers all. Love never fails. Keep love in your arsenal and you will always end up victorious.

Isaiah 54:15

"Indeed they shall surely assemble, but not because of Me.
Whoever assembles against you shall fall for your sake."

Isaiah 54:17

" No weapon formed against you shall prosper, *And every tongue which rises against you in judgment you shall condemn. This is the heritage of the servants of the LORD, And their righteousness is from Me," Says the LORD.*

No weapon formed against you will prosper. God promises it. It does not mean that there will not be weapons that will be formed against you. But it does mean that they will not prosper. When your enemy comes at you with his arsenal of weapons all you need is love. Goliath had on armor and weapons. He was big, powerful, angry and ready to tear David and Israel's army to pieces. But David had only a sling shot and a rock to go in it. Love may look little in people's eyes but it is the most powerful weapon to defeat your enemy you have. Put love in the sling shot of faith and let it go. Your enemies tactics, schemes and strategies will crumble to the ground in defeat. *"Do not be overcome by evil, but overcome evil with good."*

Chapter 7

Love One Another

1 John 4:20-21

"If someone says, "I love God," and hates his brother, he is a liar; for he who does not love his brother whom he has seen, how can he love God whom he has not seen? 21 And this commandment we have from Him: that he who loves God must love his brother also."

In many ways it is easy to love God. He is perfect. He went the distance for us and sent His Son to die for our sins. He has come into our lives and has given us every spiritual blessing and has given us an inheritance. He is always by our side loving us and helping us and the list goes on. So it is easy to say "I Love God" But the Bible clearly states you can't say "I love God" and hate your brother. You can't love God without loving one another. God requires it of us." *he who loves God must love his brother also."*

It is harder to love others because no one is perfect. So people's imperfections can end up being our focus and make it difficult for us to love them.

1 Peter 4:8
*"And above all things have fervent love for one another, for
"love will cover a multitude of sins."*

Love does not condone sin in a person's life but it is able
to look beyond the faults and see the need. Behind every fault
in a person is a need. Love will reach to meet that need so sin
will not persist anymore. When a person is digging for gold
they know they are going to come across a lot of dirt. But
they are not looking for the dirt, they are looking for the gold.
In every person's life if you look hard enough you will find
some dirt. But you shouldn't be looking for the dirt , you
should be looking for the gold in their life. Love will do this.
Love will extend grace and show mercy. Love will embrace a
person no matter what condition they are in. Love will go the
distance when others give up.

John 13:34-35
*"34 A new commandment I give to you, that you love one
another; as I have loved you, that you also love one
another.35 By this all will know that you are My disciples, if
you have love for one another."*

God commands us to love one another. He doesn't give
us and option. In doing this you will prove you are His
disciple. There have been many people over the years that
have called themselves Christians but had no love. Their
actions proved it. If we are going to paint a true picture of
God's love to the world then we must understand that our
actions speak louder than our words. If we love one another
we will prove that we are His disciples and people will see
Jesus for who He truly is.

1 John 2:5

" But whoever keeps His word, truly the love of God is perfected in him. By this we know that we are in Him.6 **He who says he abides in Him ought himself also to walk just as He walked."**

1 John 3:14-18

" We know that we have passed from death to life, because we love the brethren. **He who does not love his brother abides in death.15 Whoever hates his brother is a murderer, and you know that no murderer has eternal life abiding in him.** *16 By this we know love, because He laid down His life for us. And* **we also ought to lay down our lives for the brethren.** *17 But whoever has this world's goods, and sees his brother in need, and shuts up his heart from him, how does the love of God abide in him? 18 My little children,* **let us not love in word or in tongue, but in deed and in truth.**

Love takes action. Our words are empty if there is no action behind it. It first starts in your heart but it ends up in action. If you hate someone this scripture says you abide in death and you are a murderer. That is some strong words. Do you think God is serious about us loving one another? Definitely yes!

John 15:9,10

"As the Father loved Me, I also have loved you; abide in My love.10 **If you keep My commandments, you will abide in My love,** *just as I have kept My Father's commandments and abide in His love."*

43

1 John 3:23

*"And this is His commandment: that we should believe on the name of His Son Jesus Christ **and love one another, as He gave us commandment.** "*

Remember , to love one another is fulfilling God's commandment. If you love God , you will love others.

1 John 5:1-3

*"Whoever believes that Jesus is the Christ is born of God, and everyone who loves Him who begot also loves him who is begotten of Him.2 By this we know that we love the children of God, when we love God and keep His commandments.3 For this is the love of God, that we keep His commandments. And **His commandments are not burdensome.** "*

To follow the commandment to love one another is not a burden, it is a blessing. The results are amazing. Love always births good things in you and other people's lives. Love never fails. I can't say it enough. Love never fails. Of all the things we do love is the greatest.

1 Corinthians 13:8 *"Love never fails"*

1 Corinthians 13:13

*"And now abide faith, hope, love, these three; **but the greatest of these is love.** "*

1 Peter 4:8

*"And **above all things have fervent love** for one another."*

Choose to make love your highest and most important pursuit in life. It is the key to your future. It is the key to success in all your relationships. Your relationship with God and people.

1 Corinthians 16:14

"Let all that you do be done with love."

Colossians 3:12-15

"Therefore, as the elect of God, holy and beloved, put on tender mercies, kindness, humility, meekness, longsuffering; 13 bearing with one another, and forgiving one another, if anyone has a complaint against another; even as Christ forgave you, so you also must do. 14 ***But above all these things put on love, which is the bond of perfection."***

Chapter 8

Love and Marriage

Proverbs 27:17

"As iron sharpens iron, So a man sharpens the countenance of his friend."

Marriage is the best training ground to learn how to love. Have you noticed that two people can be so in love with each other before they get married and then after they get married they begin to fight all the time? Why is that? It is because iron sharpens iron. The only way to sharpen something is for something of equal strength or more to become abrasive and begin to remove the substance that does not belong there. I am not saying you have to be abrasive in a marriage. The differences, the flaws and the short comings automatically causes abrasion. If you have a jar filled with water but on the bottom is some garbage, as long as that jar is sitting still the water will look clear. On the surface everything will look clear. But shake it up and all the garbage rises to the surface and things don't look so clear anymore. The same principle applies to relationships. Everything can look fine in a person's life until something shakes things up and all of a sudden things you didn't know were there rises to the surface. How you deal with the garbage that rises to the surface determines how clear things will be in the future. You can either allow everything to settle down only to rise to the surface again in the future. Or you can deal with it and remove it so you won't be affected by it again. God uses people's differences to bring to the surface the things that need change in our lives.

The Self-Centered Approach

When you get married you become one flesh with the other person. It is a big adjustment. It requires adjustment. It requires for each person not to be self-centered any more. Also it magnifies the faults in each other. Nothing is hidden and all things become exposed. As long as a person remains self-centered their marriage will not work. If you want your marriage to work, quit being self-centered. Most people build a relationship on what the other person can do for them. As long as the person is attractive to them they are happy. As long their needs are being met things are great. If the person is meeting their expectations there is no problems. This is such a self-centered approach to a relationship. The marriage vows try to prepare people for the right approach but usually the vows are forgotten soon. "For better or worse, richer or poorer, sickness and health, till death do we part." Everything is good as long as things are good, but what if they get worse? Things are great when you have money, but what if you lose everything? As long as everyone stays healthy and can do their part everything will go as planned, but what if one gets sick and can't do their part anymore? What if the physical beauty changes and the person gets older and everything begins to bag and sag? People at the beginning are willing to go the distance with each other until death, but when circumstances change the commitment quickly changes. If this is the case then the relationship was not built on true love. It was not built on God's love. Love will go the distance no matter what. A marriage will fail if unconditional love is not practiced?

Maybe you have heard the term "it takes two to tango." In a relationship it takes two to cooperate and work with each other. What happens when one person is practicing unconditional love and the other is not? In most cases if one is practicing unconditional love the other person will turn around and respond to that love. If you begin to walk in God's love towards the other person and you don't see immediate results, don't give up. Jesus loves us unconditionally . Some people it took many years to realize and to respond to that love. But He was patient and never gave up on them. Some still have not responded to His unconditional love, yet He will never give up on them.

Abuse in Marriage

If you are in a verbal or physical abusive relationship get out. At least separate until the abuser can prove they have changed. You are not loving that person if you continue to allow them to abuse you. You are enabling them to continue in their sin. God does not require you to stay in a relationship like this. You can love a person and forgive them but you don't have to give them a license to abuse you. Fear of retaliation can keep a person from removing themselves from abusers. Don't let fear keep you from doing what is necessary. If an abuser does not see that there are consequences to their actions then they will continue in that behavior. Don't let them continue in this and don't be afraid to take action.

1 John 4:18
" There is no fear in love; but perfect love casts out fear, because fear involves torment. But he who fears has not been made perfect in love.."

Love Like Jesus Loves

Ephesians 5:25
"Husbands, love your wives, just as Christ also loved the church and gave Himself for her."

This scripture is a key to a successful marriage. It is not complicated. If spouses would love each other like Jesus loved and gave Himself for the church then their marriage would succeed. If we are going to love like Jesus we must discover how He loves so we can follow His example. He is God and He is our Lord yet He lived and showed the example of a servant.

Matthew 20:25-28
*"You know that the rulers of the Gentiles lord it over them, and those who are great exercise authority over them.26 Yet it shall not be so among you; but whoever desires to become great among you, let him be your servant.27 And whoever desires to be first among you, let him be your slave 28 **just as the Son of Man did not come to be served, but to serve, and to give His life a ransom for many.**"*

Jesus taught that if you want to be great you must become a servant. He not only taught it He lived it to the very end. He did not come to be served although He deserves to be served. But He came to serve and give His life for you and me. That is a big sacrifice. Husbands and wives must take on the heart of a servant towards one another. Your goal is to learn to serve instead of expecting to be served whether you feel like you deserve to be served or not. The heart of a servant will make you the greatest husband or wife.

John 13:13-15

*"You call Me Teacher and Lord, and you say well, for so I am.14 If I then, your Lord and Teacher, have washed your feet, you also ought to wash one another's feet.15 **For I have given you an example,** that you should do as I have done to you."*

A servant serves. If you are a true servant it will be reflected in your actions. If you try to act like a servant you will get tired of doing it real quick because your actions can go unappreciated and taken for granted.

Luke 17:7-10

*"7 And which of you, having a servant plowing or tending sheep, will say to him when he has come in from the field, 'Come at once and sit down to eat'?8 But will he not rather say to him, 'Prepare something for my supper, and gird yourself and serve me till I have eaten and drunk, and afterward you will eat and drink'?**9 Does he thank that servant because he did the things that were commanded him?** I think not. 10 So likewise you, when you have done all those things which you are commanded, say, 'We are unprofitable servants. We have done what was our duty to do.'"*

Husbands Love, Wives Submit

Colossians 3:18-19

"Wives, submit to your own husbands, as is fitting in the Lord. 19 Husbands, love your wives and do not be bitter toward them."

I have heard it said by many people that the scripture requires a husband to love his wife but the wife just has to submit to the husband. I say the scripture teaches us that Husbands must love their wives and wives must love their husbands. Wives must submit to their husbands and husbands must submit to their wives. As believers we are called to love one another. As believers we are called to serve one another.

Galatians 5:13

" Through love serve one another."

1 Peter 5:5

"Yes, all of you be submissive to one another."

These principles apply to all believers whether they are married or not. If we can learn to love and serve one another our relationships will succeed and be blessed. Husbands and wives are equal. One is not greater than the other. One is not superior than the other. But God has set up roles in a marriage that work together in harmony and produces unity. It is what makes a couple one flesh. We look at God the Father, God the Son and God the Holy Spirit. One is not superior above the other . They are equal, but they function in different roles.

Ephesians 5:22-33

"Wives, submit to your own husbands, as to the Lord. 23 For the husband is head of the wife, as also Christ is head of the church; and He is the Savior of the body. 24 Therefore, just as the church is subject to Christ, so let the wives be to their own husbands in everything. 25 Husbands, love your wives, just as Christ also loved the church and gave Himself for her, 26 that He might sanctify and cleanse her with the washing of water by the word, 27 that He might present her to Himself a glorious church, not having spot or wrinkle or any such thing, but that she should be holy and without blemish. 28 So husbands ought to love their own wives as their own bodies; he who loves his wife loves himself. 29 For no one ever hated his own flesh, but nourishes and cherishes it, just as the Lord does the church. 30 For we are members of His body, of His flesh and of His bones. 31 "For this reason a man shall leave his father and mother and be joined to his wife, and the two shall become one flesh." 32 This is a great mystery, but I speak concerning Christ and the church. 33 Nevertheless let each one of you in particular so love his own wife as himself, and let the wife see that she respects her husband.

Learning to love God's way is the way to go. You will never have to use the "D" word (divorce) if you love your spouse like God loves you. Unconditionally and everlasting.

Chapter 9

The Love Chapter

1 Corinthians 13 is known as the love chapter in the Bible. It describes love. It describes God's love. Spend some time reading this chapter. Meditate on the description of what love is. It will help you learn how to love God's way. Read as many translations of this chapter as you can. It will give you clearer insight to the love of God.

1 Corinthians 13:1-13

"Though I speak with the tongues of men and of angels, but have not love, I have become sounding brass or a clanging cymbal. 2 And though I have the gift of prophecy, and understand all mysteries and all knowledge, and though I have all faith, so that I could remove mountains, but have not love, I am nothing. 3 And though I bestow all my goods to feed the poor, and though I give my body to be burned, but have not love, it profits me nothing. 4 Love suffers long and is kind; love does not envy; love does not parade itself, is not puffed up; 5 does not behave rudely, does not seek its own, is not provoked, thinks no evil; 6 does not rejoice in iniquity, but rejoices in the truth; 7 bears all things, believes all things, hopes all things, endures all things. 8 Love never fails. But whether there are prophecies, they will fail; whether there are tongues, they will cease; whether there is knowledge, it

will vanish away.9 For we know in part and we prophesy in part.10 But when that which is perfect has come, then that which is in part will be done away.11 When I was a child, I spoke as a child, I understood as a child, I thought as a child; but when I became a man, I put away childish things.12 For now we see in a mirror, dimly, but then face to face. Now I know in part, but then I shall know just as I also am known.13 And now abide faith, hope, love, these three; but the greatest of these is love.

We can learn so much from this chapter. The first part of the chapter focuses on things that people do that make them look important in others eyes and in their own eyes. People who are gifted or talented are usually admired.

Proverbs 18:16
"A man's gift makes room for him, And brings him before great men."

God has gifted all of us in many different ways, but if we use these gifts without love we are making noise. In fact , no matter how many gifts and talents you have – if you do not operate in love – you are nothing and it profits you nothing.

It is possible to gain the whole world through your gifs and talents , but lose your soul.

Mark 8:36
"For what will it profit a man if he gains the whole world, and loses his own soul?"

Most people equate giving up their possessions and helping the poor an act of love or compassion. According to 1 Corinthians 13:3 , a person can do this without love and if they do this without love, it profits them nothing. Some people give to others to make themselves look good. Some give with the motivation of gaining something from it. Giving can give a person a sense of control to make things happen. But God's love and compassion is what should compel us to give. We can even sacrifice our lives for others but have not love. Love must always be the motivation in everything we do. Check the motives of your heart and ask yourself, "Why am I doing this?", "What is my motive in what I am doing or saying?

Verses 4-7 is what I call "The love check list" Let's go down this list and see if we are truly operating in love.

v.4a – *" Love suffers long"* This means that love endures and is very patient

v4b – *"Love...is kind"* Showing kindness to others is being friendly , generous and considerate.

v4c – *"Love does not envy"* Envy is being discontent, resentful and coveting others possessions or qualities.

v4d – *"Love does not parade itself"* Love will not boast or brag. A person who loves will not try to draw attention to themselves to make them look important.

v4e – *"Love...is not puffed up"* Love will not be prideful and arrogant.

v5a – *"Love...does not behave rudely"* Being rude is to act offensively, impolite and ill-mannered.

v5b – *"Love... does not seek its own"* Love is not selfish, it does not demand its own way. It is not self-seeking.

v5c – *"Love...is not provoked"* When you are provoked you react to people and situations. You are incited to do or feel something especially anger.

v5d – *"Love... thinks no evil"* It keeps no record of wrongs. It does not take into account a wrong suffered

v6a – "Love....does not rejoice in iniquity" It is not glad when evil things happen to others.

v6b – "But (love) rejoices in the truth" It is happy when right and truth prevail.

v7a – "Love...bears all things" If you love someone you will always be loyal to them no matter what the cost.

v7b –"Love...believes all things" If you love someone you will always believe in them.

v7c – "Love...hopes all things" If you love someone you will always expect the best for them.

v7d – "Love...endures all things" If you love someone you will always stand your ground in defending them.

So how did you do on your check list? Remember it is the Holy Spirit that can and will give you the love you need to succeed in every type of relationship. Keep pursuing love in everything you do and say and you will be blessed. In fact verse 8 clearly states *"Love never fails"* When your gifting and talents begin to fade away love will endure. When you don't know what to do, or what to say –choose love. That choice will never fail you.

1 Corinthians 13:13

"And now abide faith, hope, love, these three; but the greatest of these is love."

It is not bad to have faith or hope. These are good things. We need both. But love is greater. So the most important thing you can seek for your life is love. The first verse of the next chapter continues the message;

1 Corinthians 14:1

"Pursue love, and desire spiritual gifts"

It is not wrong to desire spiritual gifts, but first we must pursue love. The gifts of the Spirit must operate with the Fruits of the Spirit. They operate together. The primary fruit of the Spirit is –Love.

Chapter 10

Jesus
A Man of Compassion

Compassion is essential to healing

Many people pray for others to be healed but see no results. I have learned that the Love of God is the most powerful avenue of healing. Whenever Jesus prayed for others, the Bible records that "He was moved with compassion" True compassion is born from the Love of God. Compassion is having a deep care for another's need and pursuing to alleviate and meet that need. Faith is important for healing but even greater than faith is love.

Matthew 9:35-38
*"35 Then Jesus went about all the cities and villages, teaching in their synagogues, preaching the gospel of the kingdom, and healing every sickness and every disease among the people. 36 But **when He saw the multitudes, He was moved with compassion for them**, because they were weary and scattered, like sheep having no shepherd. 37 Then He said to His disciples, "The harvest truly is plentiful, but the laborers are few. 38 Therefore pray the Lord of the harvest to send out laborers into His harvest."*

Matthew 20:32-34

32 So Jesus stood still and called them, and said, "What do you want Me to do for you?" 33 They said to Him, "Lord, that our eyes may be opened." 34 So Jesus had compassion and touched their eyes. And immediately their eyes received sight, and they followed Him."

Mark 1:40-43

40 Then a leper came to Him, imploring Him, kneeling down to Him and saying to Him, "If You are willing, You can make me clean." 41 And Jesus, moved with compassion, put out His hand and touched him, and said to him, "I am willing; be cleansed." 42 As soon as He had spoken, immediately the leprosy left him, and he was cleansed

We must have compassion
even when we have suffered a personal loss

There will be times when you have a deep need yourself and you are confronted with the needs of others. How will you respond? Typically we would not even attempt to help others when we have a great need ourselves. But compassion will move you beyond your need. That's what happened to Jesus. His first cousin John the Baptist was senselessly murdered. Jesus love him and felt the pain of the loss of such a loved man and godly man. Jesus needed to get away , alone and deal with His loss. He wanted to go to a deserted place by himself. The multitude of people with their needs heard where He was going and met Him there. Jesus could have said "Listen, I am hurting right now, let me deal with my grief. Come back next week." Instead He was moved with compassion and ministered to the multitude of people.

Matthew 14:10-17

"So he sent and had John beheaded in prison. 11 And his head was brought on a platter and given to the girl, and she brought it to her mother. 12 Then his disciples came and took away the body and buried it, and went and told Jesus. 13 When Jesus heard it, He departed from there by boat to a deserted place by Himself. But when the multitudes heard it, they followed Him on foot from the cities. 14 And when Jesus went out He saw a great multitude; and He was moved with compassion for them, and healed their sick. 15 When it was evening, His disciples came to Him, saying, "This is a deserted place, and the hour is already late. Send the multitudes away, that they may go into the villages and buy themselves food." 16 But Jesus said to them, "They do not need to go away. You give them something to eat."

When you have compassion
you will care about the needs of others

Sometimes the need seems to great to meet. The need that is presented before us can be overwhelming causing us to conclude that we must not be the right person to try to meet that need. But compassion will compel us to do something about it. A lack of compassion will cause us to ignore it. Jesus and His disciples were presented with such a need. The multitude had followed them for three days and they had nothing to eat. Because Jesus had compassion on them He took what was provided, a small lunch enough for one person and He worked a miracle and fed 5,000 men plus women and children.

Matthew 15:32-33
"32 Now Jesus called His disciples to Himself and said, "I have compassion on the multitude, because they have now continued with Me three days and have nothing to eat. And I do not want to send them away hungry, lest they faint on the way."

Whenever you are presented with a great need allow compassion to lead you. Compassion coupled with faith will produce amazing miracles. It allows God to work in our midst. When we lack compassion we close the door to miracles. Let the Love of God fill your heart right now and be led by the Holy Spirit and you will see miracles.

Compassion will take the lead even when you are too busy

There was such a demand on Jesus and His disciples. Every day from morning to night they were pulled upon and called upon to the point that they did not even have time to eat. They needed a vacation. A retreat, something. They just needed to get a way and get some rest. They finally decided to depart to a deserted place to get a rest. Wouldn't you know it, the multitude found out and ran ahead and got there before they did. They didn't even have time to take a short nap. If we were in this situation most like we would say something like this to the multitude. " Our office hours are Monday through Friday 9-5. Come back on Monday and we will help you." But Jesus was once again moved with compassion and began to minister to their needs and teach them.

Mark 6:31-34
"31 And He said to them, "Come aside by yourselves to a

deserted place and rest a while." For there were many coming and going, and they did not even have time to eat. 32 So they departed to a deserted place in the boat by themselves. 33 But the multitudes saw them departing, and many knew Him and ran there on foot from all the cities. They arrived before them and came together to Him. 34 And Jesus, when He came out, saw a great multitude and was moved with compassion for them, because they were like sheep not having a shepherd. So He began to teach them many things."

My prayer for you and me is that we would allow the Holy Spirit to fill us with the Love of God. That we would allow Him to mold us and shape us after the character and life of Jesus. That when people see our actions and hear our words that they would see and hear Jesus through us.

1 Corinthians 13:13
"And now abide faith, hope, love, these three; but the greatest of these is love."

Ephesians 3:19
"To know the love of Christ which passes knowledge; that you may be filled with all the fullness of God."

2 Corinthians 13:14
"The grace of the Lord Jesus Christ, and the love of God, and the communion of the Holy Spirit be with you all. Amen."

Appendix
Personal stories
Learning to love God's way

The many experiences we go through teaches us many things. I want to share with you some of those stories that shaped me and helped me to learn how to love God's way. In no way have I arrived, but I have learned many things on my journey. I pray these stories will help you in your pursuit to learn how to love God's way.

I thought I was a forgiving person

I thought I was a person that didn't carry offenses. I thought that I had learned to forgive people no matter what. But God showed me differently.

In the 1970's I was a youth pastor at a church. There was a leader in the church who rose up against the pastor. This leader also had a lot of family in the church and a lot of influence. He decided he didn't like the pastor and he was going to get rid of him. The turmoil and dissention in the church became so bad that they had to call in a district official to a meeting with the church to try to mediate. The official stood up and began to talk about how we needed to love one another. The leader stood up and shouted "you don't know what you are talking about." He stormed out of the sanctuary. I saw one of young people get up crying and going after this leader. I thought I better go after him. When I reached the hallway I saw this young person saying. "Can't we just love one another?" The leader poked him in the chest and said "you don't know what you are talking about. Just stay out of this business." Then I heard the young man say "If this is what being a Christian is all about, then I don't want to be one." He ran out of the church crying. I went after him and sat down with him and explained that this is not what being a Christian is all about. In fact it was far from it.

The pastor had been so hurt through all of this he left the church and because I was on his staff I resigned also and looked for a different place of ministry. The leader got his way and all the "offenders" remained at the church.

I became an assistant pastor in another church in a different state. I had long forgotten what happened and I went on with my life. One day an evangelist came and he began to preach about forgiving others. I thought to myself, "I don't hold any unforgiveness towards anyone." The evangelist said. Let the Holy Spirit shine light on your heart and reveal any unforgiveness that is in there. Suddenly God asked me the question. "If I asked you to go back to the church you were in before would you go and would you feel comfortable around those people? I had to answer "No" Then He asked me " Do you believe I can bless those people and that church?" and again I had to answer "No" . I realized I needed to forgive them and that night I did. But God wasn't finished. The leader from that church that had caused the offense called me and asked me to come and preach for them. I didn't have those feelings anymore and accepted the invitation. I went and God blessed that service. God proved to me that I truly forgave them that night.

I could continue to give you story after story of people who have used me, abused me, stolen from me, brought false accusations against me. But God has taught me to respond in love and forgive. Because I have done this God has blessed me. I am a happy man. I enjoy life. God uses me to touch many people. He prospers me. Everything I put my hand to is blessed. Read the story of Joseph and you will see that he could have become very bitter person. So many people wronged him and he suffered because of other people's choices. But he chose to forgive and God blessed him greatly. When he became one of the highest leaders in Egypt and the original offenders (his brothers) stood before him he did not hold the offense against them but had a healthy perspective towards the offenses caused by them.

Love is the Key

It is very difficult to handle being judged by others, especially those that are supposed to be your friends, fellow Christians and leaders in the church..

Proverbs 27:6
"Faithful are the wounds of a friend, But the kisses of an enemy are deceitful."

My wife and I back in 1980 took a position at a church in Colorado. At first everything was great. Things were going well and we loved where we were at. Soon after arriving my wife became very ill. She was bleeding constantly and was not doing very well. The leadership of the church concluded that she must not be living right to have these physical problems and decided she needed demons cast out of her. They tried to do this but nothing happened because she didn't have any demons in her. Finally my wife could not take this anymore and told me she was moving back to California with or without me. I agreed we needed to move. The church in many ways was border lining on being a cult. On the outside they appeared to be good Christians but after awhile many extreme theological point of views and control issues came to the surface. I needed to tie up loose ends so she left first and I was alone in the midst of this church.

I was very burdened about what was happening and I was constantly praying and seeking God for direction. One Saturday night I went to a prayer meeting with some friends in Grand Junction. While I was praying a person came over to me and said. "I have a word from God for you, God is going to show you the key to your circumstances." I thought – The key, the key – What is the key? While I was thinking on this another person came over to me and said "God is going to show you the key to your circumstances." I received the very same word that the previous person gave me. Now God had my attention. I asked God, "What is the Key?" Suddenly I heard so clearly, "Love is the Key." Right then God filled me with His love towards these people who had judged us so harshly.

The next Sunday morning I was sitting on the platform at church during the service and the pastor got up and said, "The Bible says we should know those who labor among us." He proceeded to say some very cruel and mean things about my wife and I and I was sitting right there. The amazing thing was that I felt a tremendous amount of love toward him and his cruel words did not affect me at all. God had filled me with so much love that all I felt was compassion and peace. Love truly is the key.

Take The Sails Down

In marriage there will always be good times and hard times. Close relationships are tested and challenged from time to time. At this writing my wife and I have been married almost 35 years. During that time we have had our share of arguments. God gave me the ability to love my wife unconditionally and to diffuse arguments when they arise. It takes at least two to fight. If you choose to not be a participator in the fight you have won half the battle. It may not resolve the issue at hand but it will not continue to put fuel on the fire. But God showed me an important vision that has helped me close the door on arguing with my wife. I saw a picture of a sail boat being blown in a direction it did not want to go by a contrary wind. The sails were up and the boat continued to be driven off course. Then I saw myself pulling down the sails and the boat stopped heading in that direction. The Lord spoke to me and said the sails represented my pride. If I could learn to humble myself whether I felt I was right or not I could stop many arguments and I would not give any place to the devil. It works. I have chosen to be the peacemaker in my marriage and it has kept us from the many casualties that can be caused in relationships. What made it possible for me to humble myself? Love. Unconditional love. The love that only comes from God.

Designs Stolen By Others

God has given me many designs and ideas for products that are out on the market currently. Back in 2005 God gave me in prayer a very meaningful design for a product. (I am being careful not to mention specifics because I do not want to bring a bad name to the people that were involved.) I had this design patented and had them made. A large ministry received a sample. They loved the design. But instead of buying the product from my manufacturer, they decided to copy my design and have it made on their own. This was wrong for them to do this and also I had grounds to sue them. I contacted their headquarters and produced proof that I was the designer and that they had no right to copy it. Soon I received calls from their lawyers. These lawyers ran me around in circles. I starting to feel very upset and I was thinking about this all the time. I was not getting any resolve, so the next step was to take them to court. It was at this point that God dealt with me with this scripture.

1 Corinthians 6:1

"Dare any of you, having a matter against another, go to law before the unrighteous, and not before the saints?"

1 Corinthians 6:4-7

*"If then you have judgments concerning things pertaining to this life, do you appoint those who are least esteemed by the church to judge?5 I say this to your shame. Is it so, that there is not a wise man among you, not even one, who will be able to judge between his brethren?6 But brother goes to law against brother, and that before unbelievers!7 Now therefore, it is already an utter failure for you that you go to law against one another. **Why do you not rather accept wrong? Why do you not rather let yourselves be cheated?"***

The last two sentences stuck out to me. I would rather suffer the wrong than bring my brother to court before the world and bring a reproach to the Lord. So I decided to let it go. Then God said to me that every person that is blessed by this design, I have a part in touching their lives. That is far more valuable than any monetary compensation. I have truly forgiven and I pray for and love the ministry that did this.

Learning to love God's way is not always easy. But remember God sees everything. He knows what people have done to you or what they have failed to do for you. He knows it all.

Romans 8:28

"And we know that all things work together for good to those who love God, to those who are the called according to His purpose."

So if God works all things together for our good than why not enjoy the journey? Why not choose love in every situation? God's love is a vast, deep well that will never run dry. It is a river that continuously flows from His throne to you and me. It is a refreshing rain that will drench you. It is a waterfall that cannot be stopped. His love is never ending. His love is forever. Let Him continuously deposit His love in you.

Never Ending Love

"The LORD has appeared of old to me, saying: "Yes, I have loved you with an everlasting love; Therefore with loving kindness I have drawn you." Jeremiah 31:3

My love for you is a never ending fountain. It is moving it is fluid and it is not stagnant. I do not just say "I love you." But everything I say and do shows forth my great love for you. You are my child. I Am leading you by My Spirit. Be released into the fullness of all that I Am. Receive My love and let it spur you to action as you become a vessel poured out for My glory. Rejoice and be glad for you are my treasure. A diadem in My heart. I will form you, shape you and mold you after My image. My love for you is never ending.

Let's Pray

Pray this prayer right now. Pray it out loud if you can.

Father God, right now I ask you to baptize me in the love of God. Fill me with your Holy Spirit to overflowing. I hunger and I thirst for You. I desire you more than anything in this life. Fill me with your love. Teach me to love the way you love me and others. Give me the ability to love and forgive others like you have loved and forgiven me. I love you Jesus. You are my God, my King and my friend forever. Amen

About The Author

Dr. Rick Kurnow

Rick was raised in a Jewish home. At age 17 a Japanese friend pointed Him to his Messiah Yeshua (Jesus). Ricks life was radically changed when he invited Yeshua into his life. That was in 1974. He immediately knew he had a call on his life and entered Bethany Bible College in Santa Cruz, California. He received a Bachelor of Science degree as a ministerial major. Rick met his wife Dottie at Bible College and they were married in 1978. Together they have ministered in churches and traveled for over 35 years. Rick has been mightily used of God to impact many lives. The gifts of the Holy Spirit flow richly through his ministry. In 2005 Rick received a Doctor of Divinity from The School of Bible Theology Seminary and University in San Jacinto, California, Dr. Kurnow currently Co-pastors with his wife Dottie, Gates of Praise Worship Center in Ontario, California. www.TheGatesofPraise.org Also Rick and Dottie frequently speak and minister throughout the USA and Mexico through Kurnow Ministries International. You can find out more about their ministry at www.Kurnow.org

Dr's Rick & Dottie Kurnow

Rick is also a recording artist with the release of 3 music CD's recorded with his wife Dottie. His most recent CD is "Here Comes a Miracle." He is also the designer of the New Covenant Messianic Tallit Prayer Shawl. Thousands of these prayer shawls have touched lives all over the world. Dr. Kurnow's DVD teachings "The Biblical use of the Shofar", "The Biblical Use of The Tallit" and "Yeshua Revealed in the Passover" has been distributed all over the world and has been a blessing to many.

Rick & Dottie are the founders of Shofars From Afar, LLC a company that supports the economy of Israel by offering Jewish, Messianic and Christian products. These unique gifts can be found at *www.ShofarsFromAfar.com*

Other books are available by Dr. Kurnow:

Supernatural Is Natural – The Blessings of Hearing The Voice of God
(Also available in Spanish)

Supernatural Is Natural – Miracles, Signs and Wonders
(Also available in Spanish)

Prophetic Words For Daily Living